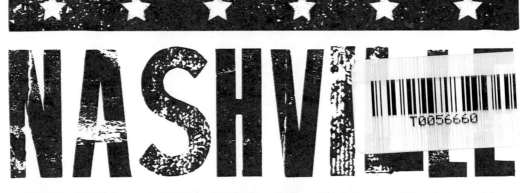

COMPANION MATERIALS

Songbook	#210616
Learning Tracks - All Four Parts (NO Full Mix)	#210830
Learning Tracks - Tenor	#210826
Learning Tracks - Lead	#210827
Learning Tracks - Baritone	#210828
Learning Tracks - Bass	#210829
Listening Demo - Full Mix only	#210824

FOREWORD

This is *NASHVILLE: Barbershop Style* … a collection of eight country songs arranged in the barbershop style that will get your toes tappin', feet stompin', and voices ringin'! From beloved ballads to fast-paced, up-tempo tunes, this folio is the perfect resource for adding a little country flair to your quartet or chorus show or performing the entire collection as a complete set of country favorites. Part-specific learning tracks have been created along with a separate full-mix listening recording to help learn the songs quickly and accurately.

This collection features classic country hits arranged by Gene Cokeroft, Aaron Dale, Tom Gentry, Rob Hopkins, Kevin Keller, Joe Liles, and Patrick McAlexander. "Forever and Ever, Amen" and "Ring of Fire" (Keller) and "Hey, Good Lookin'" (Gentry) are popular favorites from the BHS catalog, and the Patsy Cline hit "Crazy" (Hopkins) and "I Am a Man of Constant Sorrow" (Dale) from the Oscar-winning film *O Brother, Where Art Thou?* are newly published from the BHS library. "Rocky Top" (Liles) and "The Dance" (McAlexander) are both brand new arrangements created especially for this collection, and "Tennessee Waltz" (Cokeroft), as sung by legendary quartet The Suntones, appears here for the very first time in print.

This folio was created, in part, to help celebrate the 78th annual BHS International Convention, held on July 5-9, 2016, in the heart of Music City, USA. We hope "y'all" enjoy the barbershop twist on these great songs from the home of country music: Nashville, TN!

© 2016 SPEBSQSA, Inc. (Barbershop Harmony Society)
110 Seventh Avenue North, Nashville, TN 37023-3704
www.barbershop.org
All Rights Reserved. Printed in U.S.A.

CONTENTS

*Questions about the contest suitability of any song/arrangement in this collection should be directed to the judging community and measured against current contest rules. Ask *before* you sing!

I AM A MAN OF CONSTANT SORROW

From the motion picture "O Brother, Where Art Thou?"

Words and Music by
CARTER STANLEY

Arranged by Aaron Dale

Tag

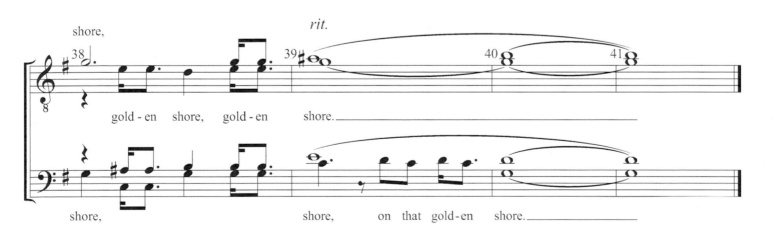

TENNESSEE WALTZ

as sung by The Suntones

Words and Music by
REDD STEWART and PEE WEE KING
Arranged by Gene Cokeroft

friend stole my sweet-heart from me. I re-

mem - ber the night and the Ten - nes - see Waltz, and I

know just how much I have lost. Yes, I lost my lit-tle dar-lin' the

Chorus 2

ROCKY TOP

Words and Music by
BOUDLEAUX and FELICE BRYANT
Arranged by Joe Liles

13

plink-a plink-a plink   plink-a plink-a plink   plink-a plink-a plink   plink-a plink-a plink

Stran - gers   ain't   come   down____   from   Rock - y   Top;

plink-a plink-a plink   plink-a plink - a   plink   plink - a plink-a plink plink   Corn____

reck - on   they   nev - er_____   will.

____   won't   grow   at   all_____   on____   Rock-y   Top   dirt's   too   rock-y   by

far.   That's__   why   all   the   folks _____   on__   Rock-y   Top   get   their   corn   from   a

Chorus 3

RING OF FIRE

Words and Music by
MERLE KILGORE and JUNE CARTER
Arranged by Kevin Keller

Chorus 1

ring of fire. ah _____

fire. _____ I fell in-to a burn-in' ring__ of

ah _____

fi - re. I went down, down, down, and the flames went

burns, burns, burns, it burns, _____

high - er. And it burns, burns, burns, the ring of

ring of fire, of fire. dah dah dah

fi - re, the ring of fire.

Verse 2

24

down, and the flames— went— high - er!

down, down, down.

burns, burns, burns, it burns,

And it burns, burns burns, the ring of

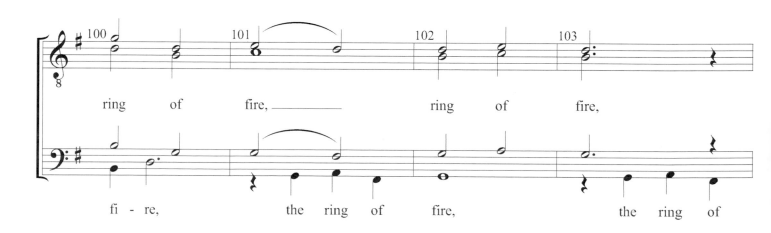

ring of fire, ring of fire,

fi - re, the ring of fire, the ring of

*Cued notes are optional voicing

HEY, GOOD LOOKIN'

Words and Music by
HANK WILLIAMS
Arranged by Tom Gentry

28

FOREVER AND EVER, AMEN

Words and Music by
PAUL OVERSTREET and DON SCHLITZ
Arranged by Kevin Keller

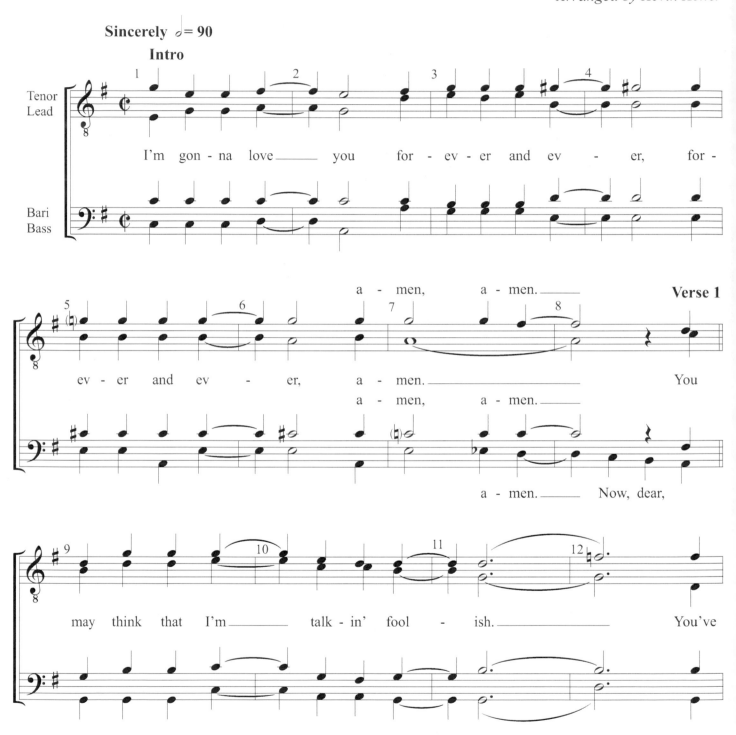

Chorus 2

I'm gon - na love_____ you for - ev - er and ev -

ends, oh dar - lin'

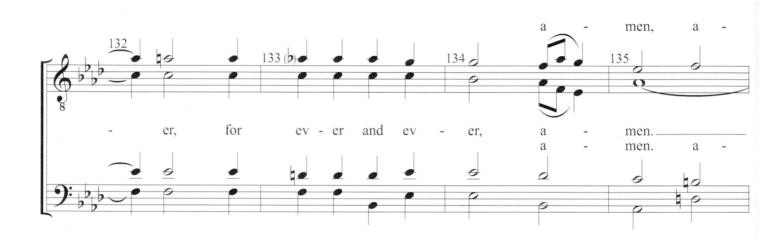

a - men, a -

- er, for ev - er and ev - er, a - men._____

a - men. a -

men.

Tag

I'm gon - na love_____ you for - ev - er and ev -

_____ men.

-er, _____ for - ev - er and ev - er, for - ev - er and ev-

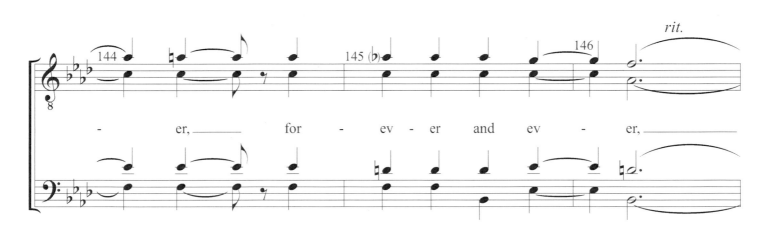

-er, _____ for - ev - er and ev - er, _____

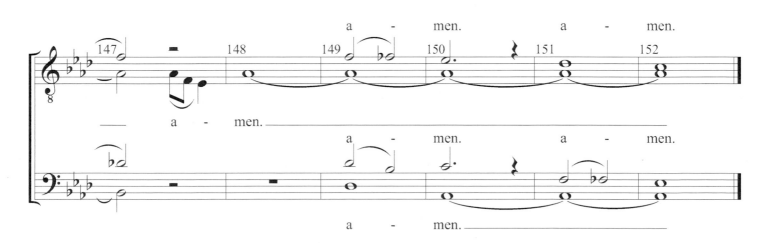

a - men. _____ a - men.

_____ a - men. _____

a - men. a - men.

a - men. _____

CRAZY

Words and Music by
WILLIE NELSON
Arranged by Rob Hopkins

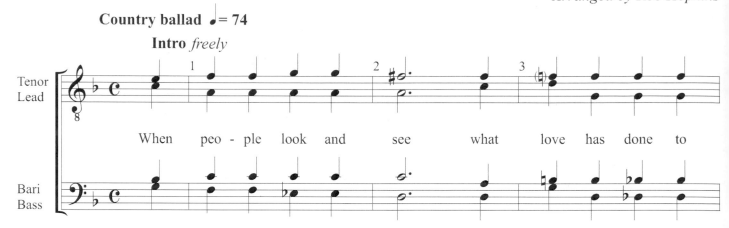

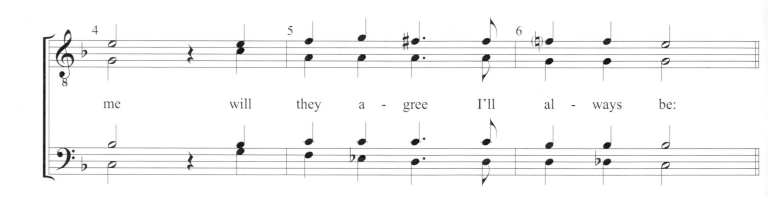

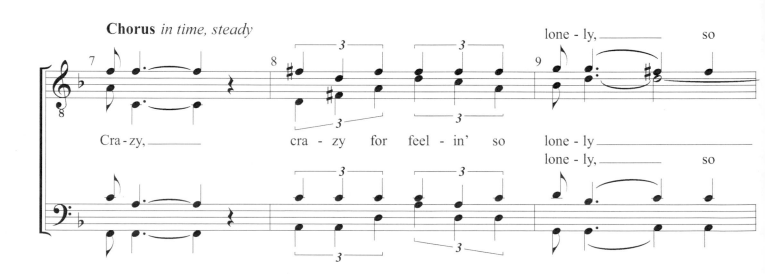

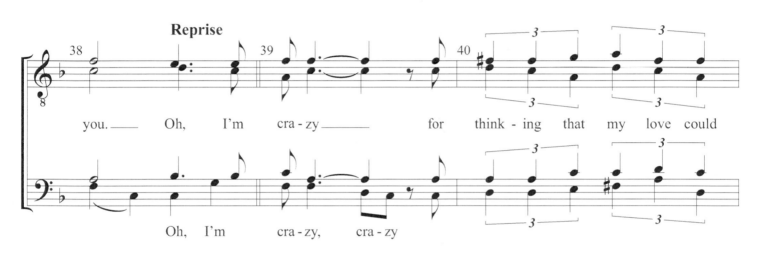

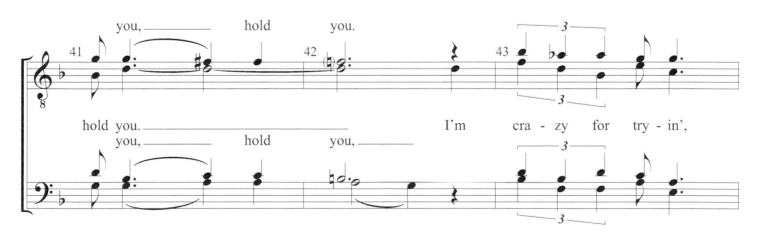

cra - zy for cry - in', cra - zy for lov - in'

and I'm

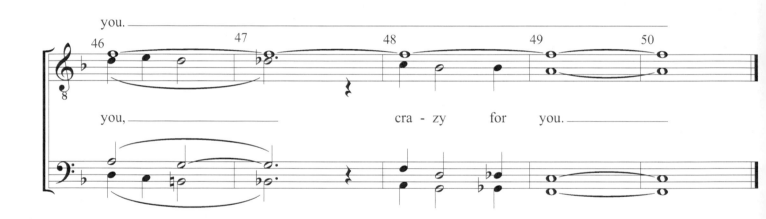

you.

you, cra - zy for you.

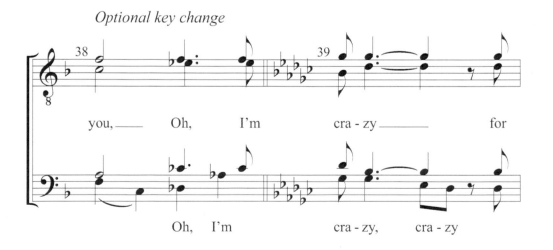

Optional key change

you, Oh, I'm cra - zy for

Oh, I'm cra - zy, cra - zy

THE DANCE

Words and Music by
TONY ARATA
Arranged by Patrick McAlexander

48

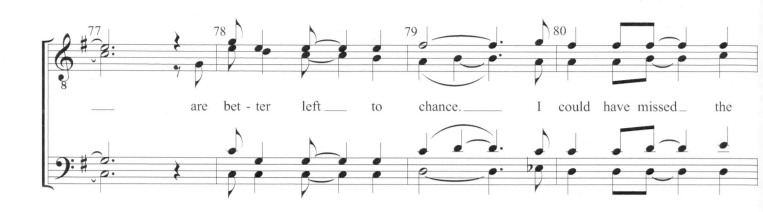

are bet - ter left ___ to chance. ___ I could have missed ___ the

pain, ___ but I'd have had ___ to miss ___ the ___

Tag

a tempo

doo doo ___ doo doo ___ doo ___ doo doo ___ doo doo doo ___ doo doo

dance. ___

doo doo ___ doo doo ___ doo ___ doo doo ___ doo doo doo ___ doo doo

doo doo doo doo doo doo doo doo